Grace Makes Badges

By Cameron Macintosh

Grace's hobby is sketching. She fills pages and pages with pencil sketches.

Then she makes her sketches into badges.

She makes animal badges
and snack badges.

You could have
a street stall
and sell that big batch
of badges!

Grace and Mum set up a badge stall outside their house.

“The price for one badge is ten cents,” said Grace.

Mitch came up to Grace's stall.
He chose a grape badge
and gave Grace ten cents.

Sage bought a lion badge and a zebra badge.

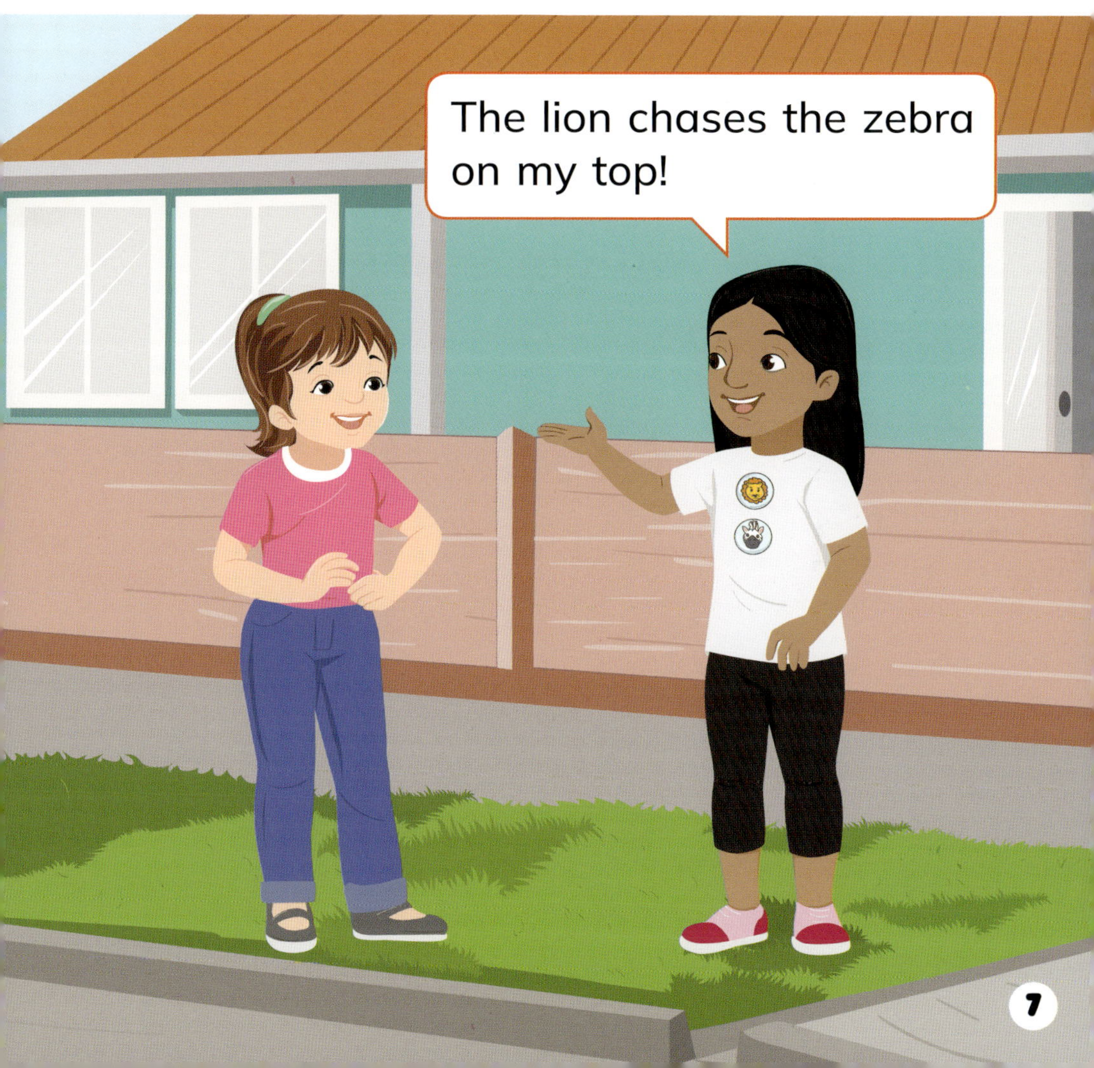

Gene had a glance at the stall.

“Is there any chance you have a space badge?” he said.

“No, I can’t draw space things!” said Grace.
“But have you got something I can trace?”

10 cents

"I have this space book!" said Gene.

"I can trace that spaceship!"
said Grace.

Grace got a page and a pencil.

She drew a line around the edge of the spaceship.

Then she made her sketch
into a space badge!

Gene was thrilled.

“This badge is so nice!” said Gene.
“Thanks, Grace!”

Mum gave Grace a nudge.

"Your stall was great!" Mum said.

"I will use all these cents to get a fancy plant for that ledge!" said Grace.

CHECKING FOR MEANING

1. Who suggested that Grace set up a stall? *(Literal)*
2. Why did Grace make a space badge? *(Literal)*
3. How does Mum feel about Grace at the end of the story? How do you know? *(Inferential)*
4. Judging by her actions, what kind of person do you think Grace is? *(Evaluative)*

EXTENDING VOCABULARY

sketches	What is the base word of *sketches*? What is another word for *sketch*?
glance	What does it mean if you glance at something? What is another word the author could have used instead of *glance*?
trace	What is the difference between tracing and drawing?

MOVING BEYOND THE TEXT

1. Grace liked to sketch and make badges as a hobby. What are your hobbies?
2. Which badge would you choose from Grace's collection? Why?
3. If you could make a sketch for a badge, what would you sketch?
4. What are some other things that people might make and sell at stalls?

TIME TO WRITE

Write about how Gene felt when he left Grace's stall with his new space badge.